NEW YORK

This book was devised and produced by
Multimedia Publications (UK) Ltd

Editor: Marilyn Inglis
Design: John Strange and Associates
Picture Research: Catherine Blackie,
Tessa Paul
Production: Arnon Orbach

ISBN 0 8317 6351 5

First published in the United States of
America 1984 by Gallery Books, an imprint of
W. H. Smith Publishers Inc., 112 Madison
Avenue, New York, NY 10016

Originated by D. S. Colour International Ltd,
London.
Typeset by Flowery Typesetters Ltd.
Printed by Sagdos, Milan, Italy.

NEW YORK

Carole Chester

GALLERY BOOKS
An Imprint of W. H. Smith Publishers Inc.
112 Madison Avenue
New York City 10016

Contents

New York State of Mind

Horns, sirens, bells — New York screams into your consciousness. People lurch and push, packing into subways, buses; decanting onto blocks already thick with pedestrians. Hurried, harassed. On their way to make another monumental decision in one of the city's monumental buildings. On their way to snatch a discount bargain from a store's never-ending sale. On their way to sink their sorrows in a dry martini.

The center of banking and communications, Manhattan sets the trend in attitudes and products. It houses the fashionably chic and the provocatively different. It is where one comes to make it, although the cost of failure is high. Another wino drains the dregs of vino tinto — New Yorkers step over his crumpled form. Purple-clothed manure collectors in Central Park go unnoticed. Perspiring joggers are considered part of an everyday scene while break dancers provide free entertainment for the '80s.

Millions work in the skyscrapers that create the canyons of the city's streets. Millions, too, live in the skyscraper blocks that look down on those very same canyons. Immigrants. From around the world — and from around the USA. Singles. Career-struck. Couples with Park Avenue penthouse money. Young families with enough to renovate a brownstone — a turn of the century house made of brownish sandstone — and to afford a nanny to walk the pram. Company VPs and international celebrities. A New Yorker is bred, not born — an Italian, a Chinese, Vietnamese, South American, Arab or Asian Indian.

In a studio apartment, WPAT radio plays soothing strains to which plants respond. In window boxes, on terraces, and even the occasional rooftop garden. When summer temperatures reach tar-melting stage, Manhattan rooftops act as 'beaches' of a city kind. A thermos of iced sangria or Bloody Marys; cassette player; and stacks of New York Times — props for city weekenders who didn't get away to Coney Island, Fire Island, Long Island.

Within the canyon's, Manhattan's 24-hour clock keeps ticking. Bars without licensing hours; coffee shops for dawn breakfasts. Stores for Cinderellas — they don't close 'til midnight pumpkin time. Late-night movies for the restless. The commuters have commuted to five borough, Jersey or Connecticut lairs, via express bus, tramway, jostled railroad or king of the highway-car. Neon-lit 42nd Street is left to the hustlers and hookers; the winking lights of Broadway, to its visitors; and the smoky Greenwich Village parlors to the locals.

They call it eclectic — patchworked cultures, colors, customs; a mundane-to-the-ridiculous mix. Anyone can be anything in New York, the Big Apple. Did the pretzel seller tell you he was once a stockbroker? Was your waitress exiled from Hollywood? Does a room with a view at The Plaza mean you've reached the top? Perhaps. Landmarks in New York, like the people, change, but the flavor remains the same.

New York dazzles at night when the lights blink on in its skyscraper blocks and sparkle across its bridges. Diamonds on black velvet. A city of neon. Billboards flash electronic messages in the city center while on the river, the small beams of passing tug boats hover and drift.

Above left Downtown, where the city began, there are still tenements waiting for restoration, waiting for the sledgehammer; offering low-rate accommodation for the less well-heeled.

Below left Manhattan has colors to suit every mood, with pocket parks and playgrounds at every turn.

Above right The twin towers of the world's second tallest building, the World Trade Center, rise 1350 feet and each tower has 100 elevators. Over 900 firms operate from this complex and thousands of office workers earn their livings here. The Center houses a hotel, shops and restaurants, including the panoramic Windows on the World, and four commercial exchanges. The observation deck on the 107th floor of the South Tower gives one of the best views of the city.

Below center Some of the world's greatest stores can be found in New York with something for every budget. This one is for the well-heeled.

Below right Near the southern tip of Manhattan, South Street Seaport is a "living museum". Several blocks of this historic area have been saved from further neglect and restored to reflect an earlier era. Within the preservation district, there are renovated houses and saloons, a market and historic vessels docked at Fulton Street Pier – all open for viewing.

This page Every year, the New York Marathon increases its numbers. Men, women, children, visitors, the handicapped—all join in, streaming across Manhattan Bridge to pant, "We made it!"

Facing page For New Yorkers, no other sport can match baseball League. The New York Mets play at Shea Stadium in Flushing Meadow Park, attracting big crowds in season (April-September). Double-headers are usually scheduled for Sundays.

Facing page below Time to concentrate in Greenwich Village. Here, or in Washington Square Park, old timers linger for hours over chess or backgammon at especially provided tables outside cafés. It's a great way to meet up with old friends, but they won't gossip 'til after the game's been played!

Above Shipping used to play a major role in downtown Manhattan's business life but now, due to the development of modern handling methods, cargo goes through container terminals like this one in Brooklyn. But cruise liners like the QE2 use Manhattan's Hudson River Terminal between 48th and 52nd Streets.

Below Most manufacturing plants and industries are situated across the bridges and through the tunnels – in Brooklyn and in New Jersey. Manhattan's own skills are of a cleaner kind – banking and communications.

Above Madison Avenue is one of the city's main arteries. Located to the east of Fifth, it is particularly noted for its numerous art galleries and antique stores, and also for the number of ad agencies. Only on foot can you travel in both directions – taxis and buses must travel uptown on the one-way system.

Below Ellis Island used to be the gateway to the US for thousands of European immigrants. Between 1892 and 1924, about 12 million new settlers were given their clearance papers at buildings on this New York Harbor island. A boat service now operates from Battery Park to the island.

This page above You name it and it happens at
Madison Square Garden, the gigantic arena/
entertainment complex on Seventh Avenue
between 31st and 33rd Streets. Many horse
shows take place here along with other
sporting events like ice hockey, boxing
matches, tennis tournaments, track and field
contests. The Garden also stages circus
spectaculars and rock concerts.

Below 42nd Street has seen many changes in
its time: some for the worse and some for the
better. In this case, it's the latter. The
glamorous new Hyatt Hotel has brought back
a touch of class to the east side segment of
New York's most famous cross town
thoroughfare.

Facing page above At the center of the
entertainment district, Times Square is a
notable Broadway and Seventh Avenue
intersection. It's here that Broadway becomes
"The Great White Way". Neon flashes from
theater marquees, movie houses and all kinds
of signs. Times Square is always busy, but at
its most vibrant on New Year's Eve for the
countdown to midnight (televised annually).
The Allied Chemical Tower stands where the
old Times Tower once stood, but the electric
news sign and lighted ball marking the New
Year's arrival have been kept.

Below Cheapest place for a decent breakfast
is a diner. They're scattered throughout the
city and, for the price, can't be beaten. Food is
basic but inexpensive and there's no worry
about hygiene.

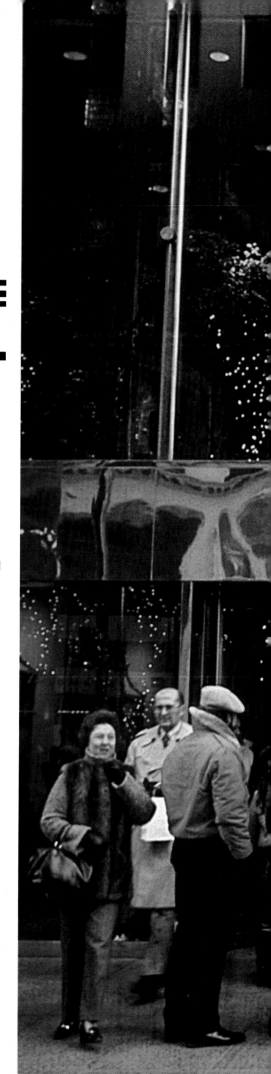

A Patchwork Culture

The riverside apartment building is still there — perhaps too old, too dirty, too established to be torn down. Through the courtyard and turn right — the door bell doesn't work. No need for spyhole or chain — she's expected. He is blonder than she remembers, sports a suit instead of jeans, says he's given up acting for good. Well, almost. There are two bedrooms, but really this apartment is studio-sized. These days there is no cat, no dog. Nor room mate. They talk of lovers past and future, bars they have known; who is alive and well and where, who is dead and buried and forgotten. Each is still looking for that meaningful relationship, but not with each other.

In an uptown restaurant, all pine and plants and trying to be French, a girl drums her fingers on the table, impatiently, as if sorry she'd given up cigarettes. She has all but given up hard liquor and red meat as well, but not her shrink.

At a party it is hard to know whose spouse is whose when everyone seems to have been somebody else's. It is possibly better, after all, to be single.

New York is a singles town. Millions of unattached (temporarily and otherwise) people live in sky-high boxes. Few were born here, but they came to make their name, fame and fortune. So-called Singles Bars on First, Second and Third Avenues in the sixties and seventies cater to them. Places to meet — someone new. Places where eye contact is the name of the game.

Some get married and stay in the city, living in security-controlled apartment blocks with watchful cameras and doormen on 24-hour duty. Security takes precedence over space. Cabs often have securi-shields between them and you, no matter how tough the driver looks.

New York cabbies are a unique breed.

Not all have half-chewed cigars drooping from their mouth. Not all come from Brooklyn or the Bronx. Not all are ill-mannered and uncouth. What they are is heavy on the horn and skilful on the accelerator when other traffic permits. And above all talkative. A fare generally pays for a life story.

New York cabbies come in a variety of shapes, sizes and ages. But no matter how young they are, their cars always seem battered. Spring-less seats — all the better for bouncing along pot-holed roads. Torn seats — to save vandals the trouble. Dented doors — when the course of true driving didn't run smooth.

Contrary to some beliefs, not all cabbies know their way around town. Not all of them speak English so well either. But then again, Manhattan was founded by immigrants and was always a cocktail of nationalities.

Just as today people come to New York to make their mark, in the good old bad old days of the early immigrants, the story was the same. And some made it big, like the Astors; Alexander Stewart, from poor Irish to millionaire; and Cornelius Vanderbilt, originally just a Staten Island ferryman.

A century or so ago it was mostly immigrants who lived in The Bowery, from Chatham Square to East 2nd Street. Today, immigrants form the very fabric of New York. But even in a new home, the old customs, cultures and cuisine tend to linger.

Shopping is a New York pastime and one of the newer places to browse is Trump Tower on Fifth Avenue. Donald Trump (who also owns a hotel) wants to take over a derelict East River dockside site to build on land reclaimed from the river bed. His plans call for a 150-storey tower to bring back the "tallest building" title to New York.

Left above In 1830, *the* place to live was around Washington Square in a fancy red brick mansion. The square, in the heart of Greenwich Village, is dominated by an imposing arch, and was the setting for Henry James' novel *Washington Square.* Today, a variety of people of all ages come here to relax, play a guitar or enjoy a game of chess.

Left below New York cabbies are a breed unto themselves but they don't all chew on a cigar or hail from Brooklyn. Many of the city's more recent immigrants, like this one, have taken up driving a yellow cab for a living. They don't always speak good English and they don't always know the way but they are, so we're told, taking classes in good manners!

This page Why so many cops turn out to be Italian, we're not sure, but a strong hand is sometimes necessary to deal with crime in these streets. Equally good at the job are the Irish who also have a liking for the badge and uniform.

This page What better place to be for Chinese New Year than Chinatown.

Facing page above left Fresh fish, meats and vegetables are sold in small Chinese community shops. The quarter is self-contained but it welcomes visitors interested in an authentic meal, rattan work or other Oriental goods.

Above right Chinatown's architecture has a touch of the Far East about it.

Below Most people speak English here, though the shop signs and street banners are in Chinese and the majority of goods on sale are of Oriental origin.

Chinatown

Chinatown begins just below Canal Street on the Lower East Side but with the influx of people from other Asian countries has infringed on 'Little Italy', its neighboring community. Several thousand Chinese Americans live here and their ranks are swelled on weekends and festive occasions when friends and relatives descend.

The chatter of the Chinese tongue; the Oriental signs readable only by Far Eastern eyes; and the exotic pagoda-topped telephone kiosks seem to have little in common with baseball and hotdogs. Chinese coffee shops are not like uptown ones: instead of coffee and a Danish it's green tea and sweet rice cakes. And in the grocery stores there may be catsup, but just as likely dried fish, ginseng and 1000-year-old eggs.

True to Chinese pattern, many stores and restaurants are family-owned and run. The greater the number of Asian faces and chopsticks, the more authentic the food. Indeed, Chinatown is one of the best bets for an inexpensive meal.

Chinatown is at its most Chinese when a festival's on. Their New Year celebrations bring out the dragon dances and parades, and the fireworks go up. But Mott Street, the main street, is worth visiting anytime. One of the city's more unusual museums, the Chinese Museum, is located on this street, housing among other things a 3000 pound replica of a Chinese imperial dragon.

Above Some of the best Italian cuisine is to be found in Little Italy, just a subway stop or two below Greenwich Village. With its Mulberry Street markets and restaurants it's a lusty neighborhood from which the stalwart older generation Italians refuse to move.

Right You can't buy the beer from a street vendor, but you can certainly buy the pretzels. Indeed, New York food stalls will grill you a hamburger or hotdog, sell you chilled soft drinks, ice cream or frogurt, or roast you chestnuts on a winter's day.

Little Italy

Italian Americans are numerous, are often cops, and live all over the place, but the first Italian immigrants settled themselves in Lower Manhattan on and around Mulberry, Hester, Broome and Mott Streets. Not surprizingly, the quarter became known as 'Little Italy'. It remains pretty hard-core Italian.

One of the friendliest districts (no bottom pinching but plenty of 'o sole mio'), it remains a fairly low-rent district. The southern Italian flavor comes through in its restaurants and cafés — terrific ice cream, pizza and all the finer points of pasta cooking. Mulberry Street is equally the street for open-air markets and festivals. Anyone looking for mozzarella cheese, Italian sausage, fireworks and street dances, should come here.

Germantown

Officially the Upper East Side area in the Eighties, it's called Yorkville, so named because of York Avenue running next to the East River. Unofficially, it's known as Germantown owing to the invasion of Middle Europeans making it their home. Accents have a Viennese or Hungarian note. Coffee houses have a European atmosphere. Food shops sell paprika or delicious pastries. Delis offer varieties of German sausages.

The main street, 86th Street, is a major two-way-traffic one, lined with German movie theatres, beer halls and stores selling continental goodies. Though it's not quite Munich and it's not the only place to buy pretzels, the oom-pah-pah bands and steins of Germany's favorite brew provide New York with yet another ethnic touch.

Above Those who don't care to pay Tiffany prices for trinkets should head to the markets. Try Ninth Avenue where antiques, bric-a-brac and even food from the world over are for sale. Browsing, if not buying, is a fun way to pass the time and who knows – there could be a bargain or two.

Left What does one put in the wok? In Chinatown you can be sure to find an exotic assortment as well as the more usual varieties. Beansprouts and mushrooms – much loved for cooking Chinese – are healthy as well as delicious.

Facing page above New Yorkers love parades – and any excuse to see a pretty girl! This parade has the majorettes fast-stepping up the avenue carrying rifles and flags.

Below Parades ... parades ... parades. This one in Chinatown heralds the approach of the Chinese New Year in late January/early February. The dragon dance is always the highlight of the event, but watch out for the firecrackers – they may do more than ward off evil spirits!

This page above A ticker tape parade is a traditional welcoming event in Manhattan. Since the dawn of the computer age, they've had to use specially-delivered, shredded paper, but the result's the same; a confetti-like cloud. This one was for the Pope's visit.

Center On March 17, any Irish American worth his salt (and there are plenty of them) marches down Fifth Avenue for the St. Patrick's Day Parade. It's one of those occasions when green is *everyone's* favorite color – even if they're not Irish.

Below Little Italy keeps its own customs and traditions and its native Italian festivals. This one's in celebration of St. Antony of Padova. There are street markets, dancing and, as always, music.

Harlem

A large proportion of black New Yorkers live in Harlem, a district that lies north of Central Park between 110th and 155th streets, river to river. The people living in the east tend to be of Hispanic origin, but it was the western quarter that was so famous for its clubs and jazz in the 1920s and 1930s. In those days, being 'out on the tiles' always meant finishing up in an after-hours Harlem speakeasy.

Unfortunately hot spots like the Savoy Ballroom and the Cotton Club no longer exist and despite some attempts to revitalize Harlem, it remains rundown and overcrowded. Its main artery, 125th Street, is no longer the place most people would care to be for a 2 a.m. binge though there is black vaudeville and a couple of jazz hangouts which do pull the crowds. The Creole restaurants fringing the district are undoubtedly good value.

Jewish New York

Jewish New Yorkers are probably the predominant ethnic group and have done the best. Between 1881 and World War I, thousands of Jewish immigrants came from Eastern Europe in search of a new world. They settled in and around Orchard Street, inadvertently turning the Lower East Side into a Jewish ghetto with a population of well over a million just in this tiny section.

Today there are more than two million Jews in New York, most of whom wouldn't be caught dead living in the Lower East Side. The well-educated, pampered Jewish American Princess (JAP for short) buys her kosher pickles from an uptown delicatessen and her clothes from Saks or Bloomingdales, not from an Orchard Street pushcart.

Today, Puerto Ricans, Cubans and other nationalities are more likely to live in Lower East Side tenements than are New York's Jews. There are modern housing projects and only a few Jewish theaters left on Second Avenue. Street trading still flourishes in Essex and Orchard Street markets, but items for sale are certainly not limited to Jewish books and religious articles.

Above Not all black Americans live in Harlem. Many of mixed and Hispanic blood now live in parts of the Lower East Side, once a strictly Jewish ghetto. History's of little concern when it's a hot day and you've got a popsicle to eat.

Center Today, New York houses a greater Jewish population than anywhere else outside Israel and Russia.

Below Who says there's no greenery in New York? In fact there are more parks than you can count, though most of them are admittedly of the pocket variety.

Above left It's sexy, it's rhythmic, and it's called breakdancing.

Above right Whatever will you find next in SoHo! It's a lively place for street entertainment, chic boutiques and loft galleries, for trendy cafés and discos.

Center Everything happens in New York – New York *is* a happening! Street entertainers might be anywhere: a guitarist in Washington Square; a violinist in Central Park; or a jazz band like this one, playing its soul out on Broadway.

Below Harlem is overcrowded and run-down, but is trying to overcome many problems.

Shopping

Shopping is a pastime in New York, the name on the boxes and bags denoting the amount of prestige. Brand names must be seen to be believed so European designers put their names or initials on the outside for New Yorkers to wear. And smart shoppers wait for the sales when Yves St. Laurent toilet seat covers are half price in Bloomingdales.

Bloomie's where the models and celebrities shop; where the scented air is as rich as some of the pocketbooks. Bloomie's myriad boutiques under one roof have accessories to furnish face, figure, table, home and office. Yet just next door, the discount store Alexander's sells artful variations of Paris models and excellent 'seconds' for the smaller purse.

Top department stores like Saks Fifth Avenue, Lord & Taylor and B Altman are great enough to have branches elsewhere. And then there is Macy's the world's largest store, taking up the square block from Sixth Avenue's Herald Square to Seventh Avenue and 34th to 35th Streets. Everything is here for those who can find it.

Shopping is commerce. Racks of clothes trundled down Seventh Avenue are evidence that this is the Garment District. New York is an important rag trade center and in this area in the Thirties, a number of wholesale fashion houses need to load up and unload. From dawn 'til dusk, dresses and suits are wheeled from block to block giving passers-by a live obstacle course.

Shopping is bargaining at the Orchard and Canal Street markets; picking over goods displayed outside shops along 14th Street; always looking for discounts. It's any-weather amusement, in the covered complexes of Citicorp, Trump Tower or the World Trade Center. It's specialized — Madison Avenue for antiques, SoHo for modern art, Lower Fourth Avenue for books, Greenwich Village for gimmicks. Generally speaking, downtown is cheaper than midtown, but whether you are looking for thrift shops or gold toothpicks, Manhattan has them all.

Evening rush hour on Madison Avenue.

Below The most practical, if not the most desirable, way to get around Manhattan is by subway. Three lines run through Manhattan: IRT, BMT and IND, all connecting every borough, except Staten Island. The express trains stop only at the most important of the city's 460 stations, while local trains make all the stops on any given route.

This page above New York store window dressing has become an artform.

Below Horse cabbies, unlike yellow cab drivers, don't supply you with the story of their life. They will, however, raise the carriage hood and give you a blanket for cold weather touring.

Facing page Bargain hunting is best done in one of the markets. Orchard Street in the Lower East Side's old Jewish quarter is one of the best for secondhand clothes.

Sale
Members Only
Reg $49
NOW 29

Changing Skyline

The skyline has been transformed since the days when King Kong climbed the Empire State Building in pursuit of Fay Wray. The Empire State remains and will always be a landmark, but for its architecture rather than its height. For it has been dwarfed since its 1931 erection by a less graceful, but taller monolith — the World Trade Center. In its turn, the latter, too, will soon be dwarfed, by some tower out to beat Chicago's Sears Tower Building's record height.

Buildings in New York rise to dizzying levels, and then are brought down. Facades change from monumental stone to shiny tinted glass. Designs stray from spired and obelisk to circled, pyramid and tiered. Tatty warehouses have become chic galleries; old markets, new housing projects. Landfills have added new streets, new parks, fountains. Villages have merged.

While bricks and mortar grow above the ground, steel goes far beneath. No more Third Avenue El, the city's overground train system. And along with the subterranean subway, subterranean shops and restaurants. Some famous steel, of course, still sees the light — the bridges like Brooklyn, feats of engineering as well as photographic attractions. And over the years, even new additions like the aerial tramway to residential Roosevelt Island, swinging perilously in stormy weather.

Glossy atriums or gold-canopied hotel fronts, though, haven't completely replaced the old. Tenements, their windows in disrepair, their walls grafitti-scrawled, their outside iron fire escapes, still stand. Terraced brownstones, freshly painted, their window boxes brimming with geraniums — are the high-priced townhouses sought after by the young aspiring professionals. Turn a corner for the church that's tucked away, a colonial mansion or a still amazing, non-skyscraper like the Flatiron Building.

Grand Central Station is the kind of place you love to hate. Commuters pour in and out. It's one of the few remaining pieces of Renaissance architecture that is also a feat of engineering and its main concourse is one of the world's largest. The terminal has two levels of tracks from which hundreds of trains travel daily.

Mid and Uptown Landmarks

In 1775, the bulk of what is uptown
Manhattan today was then mostly country,
sprinkled with summer estates and widely
separated villages. The town of New York
was Lower Manhattan with a population of
25000. By the end of the Revolutionary War,
it had not extended by much and it was
only in the second half of the 19th century
that the city scene began to approach the
one here now.

As New York expanded, so buildings
rose in height. The historic, aptly named
Flatiron Building at West 23rd Street took
over from Wall Street's first skyscrapers,
creating quite a stir with 21 storeys. The
Empire State on Fifth Avenue and 34th took
the title in 1931 when its 102 storeys made it
a phenomenon. Indeed, during the
Depression when office rents here were
unaffordable, it was the sightseers who
paid for the building's taxes.

Of historic uptown note is The Dakota
apartment building. In the 1980s we know it
only too well as the late John Lennon's
home, but it has been an illustrious
apartment block since 1884 when it was
among the first luxury ones in New York. Its
apartments ranged from four to 20 rooms
and it was named The Dakota because in
those days it was considered as far away
from mainstream New York as Dakota!

The Metropolitan Museum of Art on Fifth
Avenue is not only a fascinating and famous
museum but an architectural masterpiece
besides. The original part of it was the first
large public building to be built in Beaux
Arts style, though the present north and
south wings were added later. The high
point of Beaux Arts style was reached with
the construction of the New York Public
Library and Grand Central Station.

Most of the buildings which have given
the skyline its impact have in fact been built
post 1930. The very distinctive Chrysler
Building on Lexington Avenue, so art deco,
with its stainless steel structure and that
series of arches culminating in the tipped
point, stands out even in the midst of far
taller buildings. It belonged of course to an
automobile manufacturer so it's not
surprising that its gargoyles are shaped like
radiator caps of vintage cars, nor that the
brick designs adorning the walls are
modeled after automobile radiators.

Frank Lloyd Wright's Guggenheim
Museum design caused an awful stir, it was
too modern for its time (1959), or so they
said. Inside there is a spiral ramp which
leads from the top to the ground floor.
Visitors like it but some consider the circular
rough concrete exterior ugly.

Built in 1959, the Lincoln Center for the

Performing Arts in the West Sixties, was another building which caused controversy although few can find fault with the operas, ballet and dramas performed here. A Henry Moore sculpture and Chagall murals denote its era.

McGraw Hill Building on 42nd Street has always been a praised piece of masonry though many regretted the going underground of Penn Station to be replaced by the above-ground Madison Square Garden Center. Tongues wagged, too, when the Pan Am Building was erected in the 1960s to straddle Park Avenue, thus blocking what had been a superb view from the Helmsley Building and Grand Central Station.

Facing page The Woolworth Building on 233 Broadway. A giant name for a giant building. Until 1930 it took the "tallest" title at 60 storeys tall.

This page below The Lever Brothers Building on Park Avenue is just one of the noteworthy Park Avenue structures. Free exhibits are often on display here.

Right Park Avenue's Seagram Building has become a photographic landmark and is thought by many to be one of the city's most beautiful skyscrapers. Its bronzed tower was designed by Philip Johnson and Mies van de Rohe, and its surrounds – greenery and fountains – provide a space for office workers to take a break. One of Manhattan's top restaurants, the Four Seasons, is located in the building.

Rockefeller Center

Surprisingly, the Rockefeller Center, New York's greatest urban complex, was built during the Depression. It starts at the Channel Gardens leading from Fifth Avenue to the sunken plaza and its centerpiece is the 70-storey RCA Building. At the Sixth Avenue end of the complex is Radio City Music Hall. In the underground mall, shops and eating places give pause for thought as well as providing the best way to get from one avenue to the next in inclement weather.

Ever since it was built in the 1950s, the Seagram Building has had cachet and not just because the glamorous Four Seasons Restaurant is located in it. Its bronze and amber glass tower says it all — the epitome of international skyscraping. Another 1950s structure, the UN Building was New York's first glass walled building. The land was purchased and donated by John D Rockefeller Jr. Talking of firsts, Lever House on Park Avenue was the first metal and glass building on Park Avenue, also from the 1950s, with a courtyard, garden and pedestrian arcade.

How does a city of skyscrapers go one further? More tinted glass, more atrium lobbies, more cubist designs. Citicorp Center arose in the 1970s, sheathed in glowing aluminium but sloping at a 45 degree angle. Because of its Lexington Avenue site, it had to allow for St Peter's Church sitting under it. And in the 1980s, another complex, Trump Tower, was completed.

Above The RCA Building is one of 21 buildings comprising the Rockefeller Center. It's a classic art deco building, as shown by the details pictured and the Steuben glass panels. The RCA's lobby is decorated with huge murals.

Left When John D. Rockefeller took a lease for a midtown site in 1928, it was with the idea of building an opera house. The opera house was never built, but many other complexes were, like the Cunard Building pictured here. Its spread includes offices, restaurants, garages and arcades of shops.

Above right There is nowhere else in New York that shouts art deco so much as the Rockefeller Center, as you can see from this picture taken in the entrance lobby of the Chanin Building. It is part of the complex which takes up a full block between Fifth and Sixth Avenues and extends from 48th to 52nd Streets.

Below right Focal point of Rockefeller Center is the massive gilded statue of Prometheus by Paul Manship, backed by a fountain. It overlooks the Lower Plaza which serves as an open air café in summer and converts to a skating rink in winter.

Wall Street Area

Once there really was a wall on Wall Street
— to block off the wilderness of the rest of
Manhattan. And the first Stock Exchange
was built on Wall Street as today's is — but
then it was established under a cottonwood
tree. Wall Street area is the oldest, most
historic part of Manhattan where streets
have names rather than numbers and have
a refreshing randomness to them. George
Washington regularly worshipped at St
Paul's Chapel (part of Trinity Parish) and
former parishioners like Robert Fulton and
Alexander Hamilton lie buried in Trinity's
graveyard.

In 1789 George Washington took his first
oath of office on the site where the Federal
Hall National Memorial stands today at 26
Wall Street. The present building is New
York's finest example of Greek Revival
architecture. Today's 'Temple of Money', the
Stock Exchange on Broad Street, has a
Corinthian pillared facade, bearing little
resemblance to that very first exchange.

But to prove the area's financial worth, it
is the banks in the vicinity which are most
impressive. Citibank at 55 Wall Street, for
example, was built in 1836 as the Merchants
Exchange; the Williamsburgh Savings Bank
at number 74 was constructed in 1926 as
the Seamen's Bank for Savings; a plaque at
The Bank of New York at Wall and William
Streets tells Wall Street's history. And the
bank of banks, the Federal Reserve on
Liberty Street, is one of the world's largest
banking facilities — a city landmark with
gold vaults 80 feet below Nassau Street.

Trinity Church, Broadway at Wall Street, is
a gem of a church, a Gothic masterpiece,
albeit not the original. The first was
destroyed by fire in 1776 and the second
torn down. Down downtown is full of such
historical elements. City Hall, between
Broadway and Park Row, is actually a small
French Renaissance palace. Originally it
was faced with marble but when the
money ran out, the rear wall had to be
brownstone. Today it is Alabama limestone.

Interesting iron work and the most
beautiful houses are to be found in this
lower section of Manhattan. William Clark
House at 51 Market Street is an unusual
four-story Federal house. Colonnade Row
on Lafayette Street is made up of the last
remaining townhouses from an era when
this was the place to live and people like the
Astors and Vanderbilts resided here.
Fraunces Tavern on Pearl Street still serves
lunch as it did in 1709 when it was the center
of communications and business life.
George Washington made his
headquarters here during the
Revolutionary War.

There were tall buildings in Lower

Left The much-loved and photographed Chrysler Building is a prime example of art deco architecture.

Above It's no surprise to find a statue of George Washington in Lower Manhattan, for he had close associations with New York. In 1789, he took his oath as president on the site of what is now Federal Hall National Memorial, at 26 Wall Street. That original City Hall was where Congress adopted the Bill of Rights. Today's building stands as a good example of Greek Revival architecture, and contains a museum.

Right Trinity Church is a masterpiece of a building, a replica of an original gothic gem — the first was destroyed by fire in 1776; the second torn down. But its graveyard is full of early parishioners and its Wall Street location is yet another reminder of the city's roots.

Manhattan even in the old days, though they'd hardly be skyscrapers by today's count. For instance the Equitable Life Building, built in 1915 at 120 Broadway caused a city zoning law — its 40-storey height cut off the sky! Park Row Building, number 15, was once the city's tallest building. Its stone, glass and brick construction on a steel frame made it a forerunner of many others. The Woolworth Building at 233 Broadway remained the biggest giant until 1930.

In some ways, the whole of the downtown area is a living museum. Indeed, that was the idea of South Street Seaport where renovation has brought new life and activity to a section that was fading away.

Left St. Patrick's Cathedral no longer stands alone, dominating the skyline, but photographed from the RCA Building opposite, its graceful lines and spires live up to its title – seat of the Archdiocese of New York.

Above right The Pan Am Building was built in the '60s to straddle the top of Grand Central Station, on Park Avenue. Though few appreciated it when it was finished – it did, after all, spoil what had been a superb view of the whole of Park Avenue – it has become a major landmark.

Below right The UN Building's interior is decorated by sculpture, paintings, tapestries and other furnishings donated by member nations. Situated on First Avenue, the UN complex comprises the green glass walled Secretariat Building, the domed General Assembly Hall, the Conference Building and the Hammarskjold Library.

South Street, once known as 'the street of ships', was the center of shipping and Fulton, a major thoroughfare. Today, historic vessels are moored at the piers; Fulton's market is lively; and row houses like Schermerhorn have been rescued from neglect.

Of the churches (of which there are many), St Patrick's Cathedral on Fifth has to be the most well known, so often photographed as a reflection in the glass tower of the adjacent Olympic-Onassis Building. Designed by James Renwick in Gothic style, it is the seat of the Archdiocese of New York and was based on Cologne's Cathedral. Renwick also designed Grace Church on Broadway when he was only 25.

If it were finished, the Cathedral of St John the Divine on Amsterdam Avenue and West 112th Street would probably be the world's largest cathedral, although the Jewish Temple Emanu-El, just off Fifth Avenue at 65th Street, has a greater capacity than St Patrick's.

Trinity is not the only small gem of a church in Manhattan, but of the myriad others, perhaps it is worth a stop at St Marks-in-the-Bowery on Second Avenue at East 10th Street. A federal design in a tree-shaded spot that dates from 1779, it manages to be an intellectual center for the East Village besides being a place of worship.

protected by law.

Who would believe that the pleasant quiet courtyard with brick-front houses, Grove Court, was first built for working class men and known as Mixed Ale Alley? Some of the original clapboard used to build the Isaac-Hendricks House on Bedford Street is still visible. It is the Village's oldest house.

Residential Macdougal Alley was once stables while poetess Edna St Vincent Millay once lived at 75½ Bedford Street, the narrowest house in the Village. Of all the architecturally worthy buildings to be seen in Greenwich Village, 'The Row' on Washington Square is often considered the best. Unified by a continuous cornice, these remaining Greek Revival townhouses once housed prominent people like the Delano family and Henry James.

Above It must be the Fourth of July! Whoever lives in this tenement is a patriot, although they may well have immigrated from some other country. Tenements like this are found in SoHo, Lower Manhattan and Harlem – more often without the red, white and blue.

Left Greenwich Village was once a village outside city limits which is why it is not laid out on a grid system like uptown New York. Its streets are named, and are often narrow and twisting.

SoHo

SoHo, south of Houston Street, or NoHo, north of same, or TriBeCa, the triangle below Canal Street, are historic districts of New York, but these days they boast image, trend, fashionability. In the 1800s SoHo was a sought-after residential district, the reason why there are so many interesting buildings still left today. By mid-19th century, it was the Fifth Avenue of its day, with a Tiffany's, super hotels and theaters, while after the Civil War, it was the factories and warehouses which kept the area's prosperity going.

SoHo lost glamor in the early 20th century. Money moved uptown. It became gloomy, poor, dingy and it was only at the start of the 1960s that it was revitalized. Artists tired of the now high rent in Greenwich Village moved here, opened up the lofts for galleries and living accommodation and by 1973 the district was designated a 26-block historic district.

Today, if you want to buy modern art, chic gift items, dine in a modern setting or disco in some unusual places, head to SoHo. History buffs might take note of the numerous cast iron buildings, significant of their era and part of the city's heritage. Particular buildings to look at are 72 Greene Street with five storys and porticos; 28-30 Greene Street; 101 Spring Street; and 114 Prince Street which shows Richard Haas' mural of a cast iron front used to decorate a blank wall.

Greenwich Village

It used to be farmland — the 'Village' really was a village. A maze of winding, narrow streets dotted with pocket parks and squares and gardens. The so-called Bohemians, avant garde; the artists and the philosophers came here to live when rents were cheap and warehouses, warehouses.

Today warehouses and the garages have become expensive studios and apartments. The artists have moved to SoHo or uptown; the philosophers, abroad. But there are remnants of charm — restored mews houses, old coffee houses, offbeat theatre. Some of the landmark streets and buildings, too, are these days

The Big Apple Entertains

New York, New York — it's a wonderful town . . . Broadway Melody . . . 42nd Street. All the glitter of the stage, spangled costumes and starry-eyed talent. At night when the neon signs flash you see why 42nd Street is known as 'The Milky Way'. Its cinemas' blinding lights and moving letters show titles of sexy movies. Popping bulbs on Times Square hoardings sell products and messages. The most famous one puffs smoke to match the steam rising from the potholes, sometimes becoming an iron, sometimes a cigarette smoker. Theater posters scream out the names of stars, faces and music which may become legends.

Broadway is actually a long north-to-south thoroughfare on the West side, but it is also the affectionate term for Manhattan's theaters. To 'make it' on Broadway is the highest accolade for a performer. Thanks to super-critical critics, a show can become 'hot' or close overnight. Broadway began to make history in the 1890s and hasn't looked back. It was here that Sarah Bernhardt made her debut and here the Barrymores made theirs. It was here, too, that Ziegfeld produced his first Follies and names in lights included serious playwrights like Eugene O'Neill, and musical talents like Irving Berlin, Jerome Kern, Rodgers and Hammerstein and Cole Porter.

Intermission, time to sneak out for a quick cigarette. Life buzzes on 46th Street. A man in a swirling purple cape is entertaining the crowd with magic tricks. He wears knee-high shiny black boots and the kind of hat they wore on the Mayflower. When he passes the hat around, coins are willingly clinked into it. Theater and the sidewalk's a stage.

There are lineups at TKTS on Times Square where seats are half-price for same-day performances. But Broadway is so loved that for the poorer producers, the less known actors and the pre-Broadway tryouts, 'Off Broadway' was born. Thriving

"Give my regards to Broadway". George Cohen was the song's composer, and there's a statue in his honor on Times Square. Broadway, New York's most famous artery, glitters with theater marquee lights and flashing neon. Broadway *is* entertainment.

This page left Radio City Music Hall is an art deco showcase that managed to survive the sledgehammer. Pictured here is the Ladies Powder Room painted by Yasuo Kuniyoski.

Below Broadway theater doesn't come cheaply, but those who are prepared to line up at the TKTS booth on Times Square may get same day theater tickets for half price – if there's availability. It could mean the chance to see a hit as good as *42nd Street*.

Facing page above Shops and stalls in the Broadway area always have a stack of hit show souvenirs. You can find badges, posters, records – but the most popular buys are T-shirts promoting hits like *Cats* and *Fame*.

Center The bright lights of Broadway. That's entertainment!

Below Radio City Music Hall is the home of New York's famous precision-dancing, high-kicking Rockettes. This chorus line's routines are the high point of spectacular revues staged here. Radio City, part of the Rockefeller complex, can hold as many as 6000 people and has a three-level revolving stage. As well as revues it's a showcase for concerts and special performances all suited to family entertainment.

in Greenwich Village, the theaters are generally far smaller than their uptown counterparts but these days performances are polished. When 'Off Broadway' became expensive, 'Off Off Broadway' was born in even more intimate theaters where actors often mix with audience after a show. 'Godspell' and 'Chorus Line' both saw the light of day in this area before they became the lights of Broadway.

Long before there was Hollywood, movies were made in New York. This is a city where theaters have not become bingo halls though they may have become seedy and tatty. The huge 42nd Street cinemas concentrate on the sinful and sordid; neighborhood places may be best for golden oldies; and the East Fifties and Sixties for first-run films. Movie festivals, art and special-interest films are screened in scattered theatres, a few of which show exclusively gay films.

But for spectacular entertainment for the whole family there is Radio City Music Hall, home of the Rockettes, New York's famous chorus girls. Radio City, a Sixth Avenue art deco palace capable of holding over 6000 people, was rescued from the sledgehammer by public demand and a cash injection. Gone are the days when you could see a film and a stage show for the price of your ticket, but in a city where landmarks fear for their existence, Radio City, over 50 years old, is a cherished survivor.

Barbra Streisand first became noticed singing in a dim and smoky New York club. There are many of them: small and intimate piano bars; a folk or country and western club; a jazz parlor or showcase club like Catch a Rising Star and Improvisation where young hopefuls work hard to get patrons to listen. Places to catch a name before it is one. Something different.

The beat goes on 'til maybe 3 or 4 a.m. The beat of reggae or samba; the beat of hard rock and disco; the mournful beat of jazz. Jazz has once again captured the city, especially in the Village and beyond. The famous Gate and Vanguard go on but a host of new names provide the strains and sometimes food. Discos come and go. Yesterday's trend-setter may be tomorrow's parking lot.

The Pepsi generation, now beyond the Pepsi age, have rediscovered sensual dancing. High rollers head across the River to Atlantic City to darkened gambling dens where Sinatra sings, and to video-filled luxury suites. But entertainment of all other kinds is right here: classical concerts and poetry readings; opera and drama; modern ballet and Shakespeare in the Park. New York has it all.

Above right The Metropolitan Opera House is part of Lincoln Center. Main opera season is September to May with other offerings during spring and summer. The white marbled Lincoln Center provides a home for all the city's principal cultural groups. Other buildings surrounding the fountained plaza include the New York State Theater and Avery Fisher Hall.

Below right The Cloisters at Fort Tryon Park is a unique museum that incorporates parts of five authentic medieval monasteries. It is run by the Metropolitan Museum of Art – donations are requested in lieu of an admission fee. Soothing medieval music and an appealing herb garden are free bonuses.

Left An amazing collection of artwork covers all periods and all civilizations in the Metropolitan Museum of Art. Pictured here is an Oriental courtyard inside the museum.

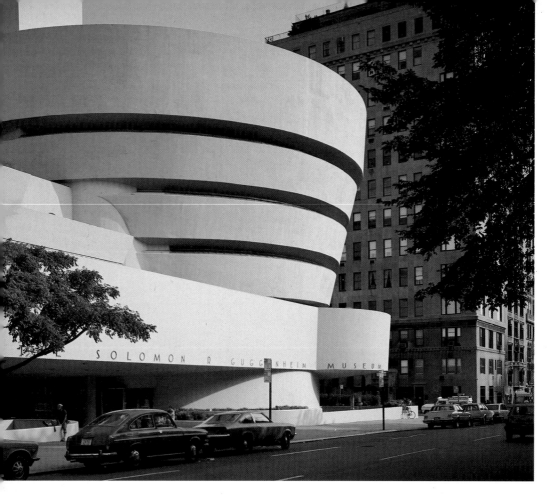

Above The off-beat design of the Guggenheim Museum caused some concern when it first opened, but Frank Lloyd Wright's building is now an attraction in itself, even without the artwork it contains. To see the 19th and 20th century paintings, visitors take an elevator to the top, and stroll down a sloping ramp that coils its way seven stories down.

Below The Metropolitan Museum of Art was the first large public building in New York to be constructed in the Beaux Arts style. Its north and south wings have since been added, giving this celebrated museum even greater grandeur.

New York has more than 130 museums ranging in size from miniscule to massive. Most are open six days a week. Even though it is spread over some several acres in Central Park, the Metropolitan Museum only has room for about a third of its permanent collection. Some other famous museums include the Frick Collection, a small museum with a nice collection of Gainsboroughs, Reynolds and Constables. The finest collection of American Art in the 20th century is housed in the Whitney on Madison. And in the Guggenheim — the strange Frank Lloyd Wright building — are collections of late 19th century and early 20th century abstract art. Further along of course, is the Museum of Modern Art which has an enormous collection of modern works. The American Museum of Natural History in Central Park is the largest institution in the world devoted to the natural sciences.

Above Affectionately referred to as "The Met", this museum contains the largest, most comprehensive collection of Egyptian, Greek, Roman, Near and Far Eastern, European and pre-20th century American art in the western hemisphere. Having "tea at the Met" is almost as much of a must as viewing the works of art.

Right Fascinating 19th and 20th century paintings line the walls of the Guggenheim Museum, designed by Frank Lloyd Wright.

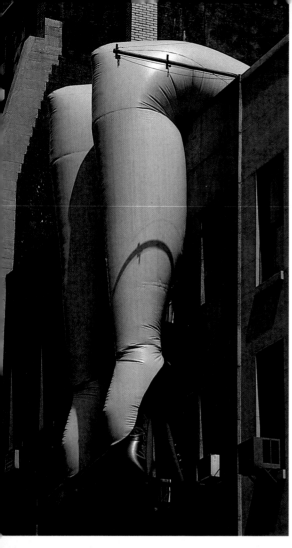

This page above left The Museum of Modern Art is about as up-to-date on art as a museum can be. Inside is one of the world's greatest collections of modern art, including over 400 Picassos, and many other paintings by artists such as Matisse, Chagall, Rousseau, Monet and Lautrec.

Above right Focal point of the World Trade Center's plaza is this sculpture called "Three Red Wings", designed by A. Calder.

Right High rise towers they may be, but many of Manhattan's skyscrapers are designed with plazas, filled with greenery, and decorated with murals or sculptures. This particular piece of work is located in front of the Solow Building on 57th Street.

Facing page Who says New Yorkers don't appreciate art?

Below A decorative addition to the World Trade Center.

Greening the City

"Can't see you now, it's tennis practise," she says. Last year it might have been squash; the year before, skate boarding. Jogging, with the addition of plugged-in music, remains. Sport is a fetish, something the New Yorker gets heavily into until she drops it.

Roller skating is less likely to knock you down on Fifth Avenue than it was at the beginning of the 1980s when it was an 'in' craze, but there are skates and rinks — some say the Roxy is the best — with skates for rent, lessons and parties. Ice skating, for those who can and those who can't very well, brings a variety of age groups out to the Rockefeller Center rink in winter. Normally, this is an open plaza with outdoor restaurants but at the end of the year, it is iced over; the skates go on and the twirling begins.

Apart from Central Park, most other participant sports are only possible once across the bridges or through the tunnels to Brooklyn, Queens, the Bronx, New Jersey, and beyond. Spectator sports, on the other hand, could mean lining Manhattan's main thoroughfares to watch the annual Marathon; taking a hamper to Central Park on a Sunday; or an uptown subway to Yankee Stadium; or paying a visit to Madison Square Garden. Yankee Stadium is for baseball enthusiasts. Madison Square Garden is for lovers of basketball, track and field or wrestling.

The easiest spectator sport is to watch TV, not necessarily at home. Many bars and lounges have a TV so that no game has to be sacrificed for those with the price of a beer or martini.

Brooklyn's Botanical Garden shows 50 acres worth of glorious blooms, trees and exotic plants. It isn't necessary to take a trip to Washington DC to see flowering cherry trees — there's a beautiful display right here.

Parks

In spite of the stone canyons, over 12 per cent of the city is made up by parks and gardens. Official statistics claim there are 572 parks, 800 playgrounds, and 350 squares, triangles and malls in NYC so the idea of greenery is not so far-fetched. Some of these unexpected patches are ancient, some recently created. Though most are small, they are a delightful find amidst the tinted glass and chrome edifices for which New York has become famous.

Who could believe that the West Village was once farmland? But it was, and this part of the city, not built on a grid system, has kept a number of its park features. Abingdon Square at Hudson Street near Bank Street, for example, designed by William Hewlett. Or right at the tip of Manhattan, as far as you can go, are Bowling Green and Battery Park. Bowling Green was the city's first park, the place where Peter Minuit made his outstanding purchase of the island. A place which has served as a cattle market, a parade ground and indeed where the 18th-century Dutch burghers played bowls. Most of the original fence encloses this patch of green, and is a city landmark, but the equestrian statue of King George III was broken up and scattered by angry colonists at the outbreak of the War of Independence.

Battery Park, favored on warm sunny days, takes its name from a row of guns placed along the original shoreline (now State Street). Land-fills have turned it into a 22-acre verdant stretch from which to regard Castle Clinton, once one of three forts built in the harbor for defense purposes during the 1812 War. In those days, it was 300 feet offshore; today it is on the esplanade. From the esplanade, Ellis Island, Liberty Island and Governor's Island are all visible, and from the terminal near Battery Park, the ferries chug their way to Staten Island.

Left Central Park is a great place to escape the grimy canyons of New York. You can picnic, be sporty or listen to a concert. But stay away at night!

Right There are miles of pathways in Central Park designed for walking or riding. Organized nature rambles and guided springtime walks are conducted by the American Museum of Natural History.

A lunchtime picnic in New York? Why not? Sandwiches and thermos jugs are commonplace in Bryant Park just behind the New York Public Library between 40th and 42nd Streets. And lunchtime picnickers decorate the benches in City Hall Park at Broadway, Park Row and Chambers Street. Somewhere restful? Gramercy Park at 23rd Street at Lexington Avenue is private but leafy. Little Greenacre pocket park (51st Street between Second and Third Avenues) offers a pretty waterfall and sitting area. Another gem of a vest-pocket park is Paley on 53rd Street between Fifth and Madison. Built by William S Paley, founder of CBS, in memory of his father, this retreat is much loved by New Yorkers.

The whiff of hash, illegal as it is, is in the air at Union Square (East 14th and Broadway) where the down-and-outs and drug dealers lurk. For fun without fracas, Washington Square Park is more reliable. An eclectic assortment gathers here; New York University students playing a guitar or two; elderly village residents bent over chess tables; strong-limbed roller skaters jiving to private strains of music; mothers with babies in strollers around the fountain.

Left Trinity Place steps.

Below Energetic visitors can hire horses from the Claremont Riding Academy in Central Park to trot along five miles of bridle paths. Other pathways are solely for the more leisurely pastime of walking.

This page What better way to spend a Sunday afternoon than a picnic in the park? New Yorkers who can't afford Tavern on the Green's restaurant prices, bring their own food, flop under a tree, watch a ball game or listen to music.

Facing page above Central Park is at its most colorful in the fall when the trees turn red and gold. Though it is well patroled by police it's best to stick to the central area and not walk there at night.

Below The most pleasant way to take the air of Central Park is by horse-drawn carriage. Rosette-bedecked horses and carriages, supplied with blankets for winter riding, can be found lined up in Grand Army Plaza, opposite the Plaza Hotel.

In the quiet neighborhood of Gracie Mansion, formal residence of NYC mayors, outdoor concerts are often given in Carl Schurz Park extending from East End Avenue to the East River, between 84th and 89th Streets. All is tranquil, too, in Fort Tryon Park (Broadway and 192nd Street), whose beautiful centerpiece is The Cloisters museum. By way of contrast, and noise, two busy intersections with places to sit are Madison Square Park (23rd and Fifth) and Herald Square, a landmark triangle near Macy's.

The clip of horse-drawn carriages through Central Park's glades is magic to some. The horses, however, decked with rosettes and ribbons, are used to the circular tour. In winter, couples snuggle into blankets. Promises and proposals are made this way. Central Park on a weekend can be like a fun fair. Musicians, jugglers, amateur entertainers of all kinds attract a cluster of people. Sweat-banded athletes and short-shorted cyclists flex their muscles. The less energetic flop under trees to watch a baseball game. Brightly colored kites fly and model boats battle the ponds.

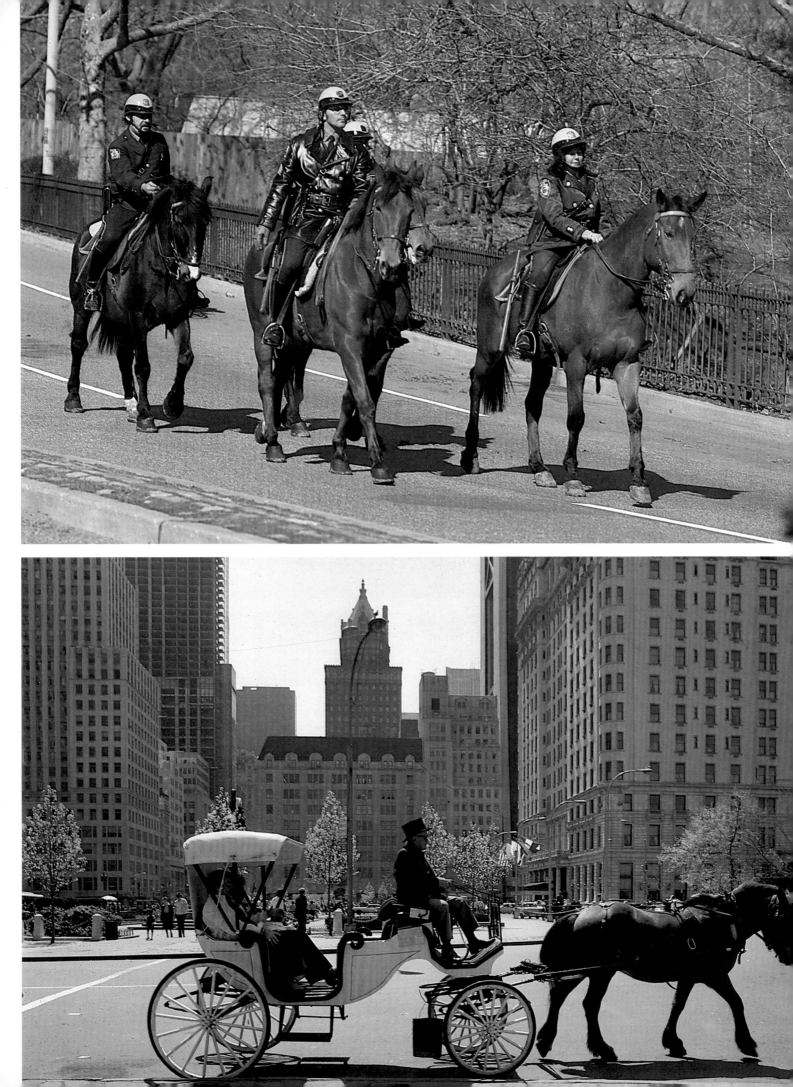

It was the 19th century intellectuals who saw the need to reserve part of the inner city for parkland. They perhaps did not foresee the dangers of muggers and rapists who use darkened niches of the park for their own purposes, and have given this magnificent park its uneasy reputation.

But in summer, when Shakespeare in the Park plays and open-air concerts abound, most of the park is populated and the atmosphere joyous.

Fishing is possible at the 72nd Street fresh water lake. Nature rambles take part centrally and guided springtime walks are conducted by the American Museum of Natural History. Players of field hockey, football and handball are welcomed and the park is one of the few places where horseback riding is possible. Despite the fact there's rarely much snow in winter, winter sports in the park run the gamut from skating to sledding to skiing.

The Central Park Zoo has its own cafeteria and the Fountain Café at Bethesda Fountain in the middle of the park is a good rendezvous point but the most elegant meeting spot is Tavern on the Green. It is a place to make a lunch date if you want to impress a visitor, but then again New York is full of places to dazzle and delight no matter how many times you visit.

Above Innumerable sports are possible in Central Park, even in winter. Skating on the lake, as pictured here, is one of the favorite pastimes.

Below left No need to leave the city to try tobogganing. When there's enough snow, no one has to go further than Central Park to enjoy winter sport fun.

Below right Winter weather can bring heavy snowfalls to Manhattan, but the city is well used to it and organized at clearing it away. Snow plows work day and night to keep the city's traffic on the move, and the commuters commuting!

Sundays in New York inevitably mean brunch. In the glamorous setting of the Waldorf Astoria where the table is laden with exotic fruits, breads, cold meats, salmon; and hot trays offer eggs, bacon, sausages and hash browns. In a small crowded Upper East Side restaurant where you can order Eggs Benedict and as many Buck's Fizzes, Screwdrivers or Bloody Marys as you can drink. All for the same price. For most New Yorkers, brunch is around noon, 1 pm or 2 pm when the *New York Times* has been read from the comfort of bed. For some it will be the ideal follow-up to the jog around the park.

New Yorkers don't necessarily look for bargains but they like a good deal. The all-you-can-eat at a fixed price concept brought in the salad bars where what is supposed to be a side dish can become a main one. Brew and burger chains charge for the meat and throw in the beer for free. Diners advertise coffee, juice, eggs and muffins for one incredibly low price and you don't have to worry that this is a greasy spoon — hygiene is an American priority, even in grimy New York.

The large paper bag doesn't contain just regular popcorn. "Take your pick," she says. Handfuls of chocolate-flavored popcorn are followed by avocado, an unidentifiable spice and others. They come from a hole-in-the-wall fast-food outlet in the Fifties. The latest thing from the town which loved frogurt and brought the kids up on hotdogs.

Fast food is everywhere. Street carts dispense franks and burgers, ice cream and soft drinks. Street stalls sell varieties of nuts and candy. Kiosks serve paper cups of fresh orange juice. In winter chestnut sellers roast their wares over charcoal on practically every street corner.

Weekend West Side food markets offer tastes from around the world: souvlaki, Middle Eastern kebabs, samosas. So do the thousands of restaurants: soul food with black-eyed peas; Creole with gumbo; vegetarian with nut cutlets; Latin American with ceviche; fondues, strudels, ragouts. Or even indigenous specialities: New York prime rib served with a baked potato with all the trimmings; better chopped liver than in Israel; better pizzas than in Italy; larger than life sundaes and Irish coffee that's topped with whipped cream.

Central Park has a zoo, skating rink, boating lake, riding school and restaurants. New Yorkers ride, jog and relax here on Sundays, and, in summer, free outdoor concerts are often held.

Above Battery Park is right at the southern tip of Manhattan. It takes its name from a row of guns placed along the original shoreline. Castle Clinton here was one of three forts built to defend the harbor during the 1812 war. At the time it was 300 feet offshore – today it is on the esplanade. From Battery Park, there are magnificent views of both the city, looking one way, and the Statue of Liberty, looking the other.

Below left The nearest beach to New York is Coney Island. Full of summer action, Coney Island's amusement park gets into swing and Nathan's hot dogs are a lunch-time treat.

Below right Boat tours are a comfortable way to see the city. Since New York is an island, the tours can circle it allowing close-up views of the skyline landmarks and the docks. The most popular tour is with Circle Line – a three hour circuit. But the Hudson River Day Line also operates trips on the Hudson River from the city to Poughkeepsie.

Facing page In summer, city dwellers head for the beaches of Long Island, one of New York's five boroughs. Though the areas closest to Manhattan are primarily residential, out at Montauk (pictured) at the end of the Island there are windswept dunes and boating docks.

This page above The view of the Manhattan skyline from the harbor is magnificent.

Below Fire Island is well-known for its summertime gay community who tend to gather around Cherry Grove, but it's also noted for the stunning beaches and scenery. Pictured here is Fire Island State Park where it's possible to fish from the pier.

Major Attractions

1 United Nations Headquarters Take the guided tour which sets out every fifteen minutes. The Secretariat building is a classic of its kind, with 39 floors of white marble and glass without a break. It contains stunning works of art and rooms donated by the different nations. If you're lucky you'll be able to obtain a ticket for a UNO debate.

2 The East Village Below 14th, from Broadway to Second. The centre of the Village is the sprawling Public Theater at Astor Place, at the head of the Bowery. Deliberately less trendy and active than its richer namesake to the west, there are some terrific theaters, clubs, shops, cheap eats and street life – from aging hippies to green-haired punks. An area definitely on the way up.

3 The Museum of the City of New York On Fifth Avenue, the museum shows all aspects of life in the city, depicted in paint, print, film, sculpture, design and artifacts. There's also an ever-changing multi-media show.

4 The Frick Collection A wonderful mansion on Fifth Avenue, built in 1913, housing the family and now home to the extraordinary collection built up by Henry Frick. The house is in exquisite condition and the rooms off the dramatic central courtyard contain paintings by Gainsborough, Fragonard and Turner amongst others. Known as the most beautiful small museum in America.

5 Boat Trips The Staten Island Ferry runs night and day and cost 25 cents, return free. On the trip you'll see the Statue of Liberty on its island, and the classic view of the end of Manhattan. There's also a round-the-island trip.

6 Harlem There are safe, guided tours through this district which is now shockingly overcrowded, overpriced and underemployed. It's not a pretty district, but it's interesting to see just why this area is so stressful.

7 Greenwich Village The most famous neighborhood in New York, it has provided inspiration to artists writers, musicians – and has acted as a springboard for those who are famous simply for being famous. Stroll along the streets, sit in the bars, coffee houses and clubs and pick up on the most innovative talk.

8 SoHo The center of American art, with around 80 galleries to browse in, it is also home to the artists themselves, along with actors, writers and the demi-monde, inhabiting fashionable converted lofts. The street life is correspondingly exciting – watch for famous faces as you explore the bustling boutiques and bars.

9 Little Italy As the name suggests, a microcosm of Italy proper. Here you will find a greater selection of pizzas than you dreamed possible, along with delicatessens offering a bewildering range of salamis and delicious home-made pasta.

10 Chinatown A small island of the Orient afloat in New York, Chinatown has shops stacked high with Chinese goods crammed cheek-by-jowl with restaurants. Mouthwatering Peking Ducks turn slowly in the windows and delicate regional specialities are on the menus. A perfect place to visit for an afternoon snack of dim sum after a brisk autumn walk in Central Park.

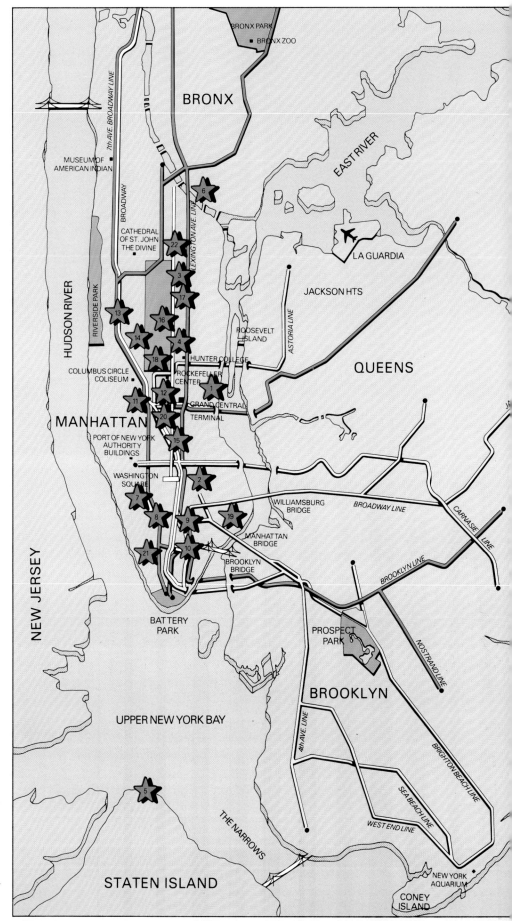

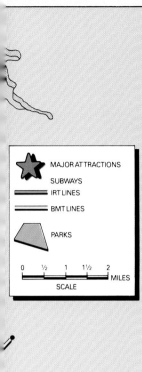

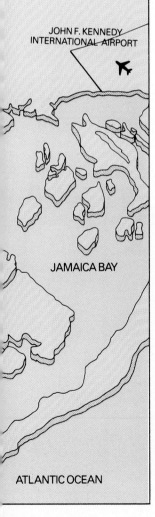

MAJOR ATTRACTIONS

SUBWAYS

IRT LINES

BMT LINES

PARKS

0   ½   1   1½   2
                    MILES
SCALE

JOHN F. KENNEDY
INTERNATIONAL AIRPORT

JAMAICA BAY

ATLANTIC OCEAN

11 Times Square This famous, or infamous, square is well worth a visit to experience the seedy side of New York. Nevertheless, it is sufficiently crowded and well-patroled to be quite safe for the onlooker.

12 The Algonquin is the most civilized and elegant hotel in New York – it once played host to Dorothy Parker, Robert Benchley and the rest of the "Algonquin Round Table" as they exchanged gossip – malicious, witty and literary – between its paneled walls. Arrange to meet a cultured companion here, sip a sophisticated drink and soak up the atmosphere.

Radio City Music Hall This marvelous art deco palace has recently been given over to extravagant musical shows and concerts. Built in the 1930s, it can seat 6000 people. The stage, of staggering size, has an extraordinary capacity for special effects.

The Museum of Modern Art is to 19th and 20th century art what the Metropolitan is to earlier periods – a comprehensive, exciting and imaginative collection unequalled anywhere in the world.

13 Broadway The very words "Broadway musical" are synonymous with the best in musical theater. This is the home of big stars and big shows, and you should take the opportunity to turn the myth into reality.

14 Lincoln Center This vast, ultra-modern complex is the center for Manhattan's music and dance, and includes four major auditoriums as well as another half-dozen venues. Most well-known and prestigious is the Metropolitan Opera House, where you can find the very best performances of classical music in America.

15 Madison Square Gardens Here you will find everything from hockey to rock shows. Its vast space can, and does, accommodate almost every sort of public gathering you care to mention.

16 Metropolitan Museum of Art This fabled museum has the wealth and style to put on the sort of exhibitions now prohibited by cost to smaller museums. The Metropolitan has 234 galleries, making it an encyclopedia of art.

17 The Guggenheim This Frank Lloyd Wright structure houses an immense collection of mostly late 19th and early 20th century abstract art. First opened in 1959, its outlines caused a sensation but are now a city landmark.

18 Central Park Everyone knows something about Central Park. Mingle with the joggers, the muggers, the breakdancers; drop in at an open-air theater or hire some skates; you haven't really seen New York until you've tried Central Park.

19 Katz's This huge Jewish delicatessen opened in 1888 and has had diners jostling for the 300 seats ever since. A visit here is a vivid and fascinating experience which adds up to far more than just a delicious kosher meal.

Orchard Street At the other end of the scale, Orchard Street on Sundays has some authentic designer fashions at unbelievably low prices in amongst a rag trade bonanza of clothes of every sort, style and quality.

20 The Empire State Building The original skyscraper. Go up to the 102nd floor and see the city laid out below you in all its bustling splendor.

21 The World Trade Center After the Sears Tower in Chicago, World Trade Center is the tallest building in the world. See the panoramic views from the top floor – or stand at the bottom and try to see the top!

22 Fifth Avenue One of the finest avenues for shopping in the world. Here you will find the legendary Saks, Bonwit Teller, and Tiffanys along with many French and Italian shops offering exclusive fashions. An immensely exciting place to window shop, hunt for bargains, or treat yourself to the best.

Multimedia Publications (UK) Limited have endeavored to observe the legal requirements with regard to the rights of the suppliers of graphic and photographic materials.

Picture acknowledgements:
Bruce Coleman Limited front cover, 9 bottom left, 13 top, 20, 27 center, 39 bottom, 50 top left, 52-53, 57, 59 top, 61, 62, 66 **Camerapix Hutchison** 21 top left, 27 top right, 32, 37 bottom, 50 top right, 51 bottom, 56-57, 65 top, 67, 68 bottom **Colorific** 8 bottom, 10, 11, 14 top, 14 bottom, 15 bottom, 43 left **Daily Telegraph Colour Library** 4-5, 15 top, 22 bottom, 24 top, 33 bottom, 35 right, 45 left, 45 bottom, 55, 62-63, 65 bottom **Angelo Hornak** end papers, 30, 31, 32-33, 33 top, 34, 44 top **Image Bank** back cover, 1, 13 bottom, 38, 39 top, 44 bottom, 49, 51 top, 54, 59 bottom, 60-61 **New York Convention and Visitors Bureau** 9 bottom right, 16-17, 42 bottom **The Photographers Library** 6-7, 8 top, 9 top, 12 bottom, 40-41, 46-47 **The Photo Source** 2-3, 28-29, 36, 42 top, 48, 48-49, 64-65 **Rex Features** 24 bottom, 25 top, 27 top left **Vautier-de Nanxe** 18, 19, 21 top right, 22 top, 23 top, 23 bottom, 25 bottom, 26 top, 27 bottom, 37 top, 45 top, 50 bottom, 58, 68 top, 69 **Vision International** R Brook 25 center, Explorer 21 bottom, Explorer/J Couran 26 bottom, Explorer/B Moreau 26 center, Paulo Koch 12 top, 35 left, 43 right